This Rock Climbing Log Book
Belongs to

_____

_____

Rock Climbing Log

Date	Time	Name of Climb

Grade	Location	Route	Length

Attempts	Achieved	Partners

Strength	
Weakness	

Beta

_____

_____

_____

_____

Notes

Rock Climbing Log

Date	Time	Name of Climb

Grade	Location	Route	Length

Attempts	Achieved	Partners

Strength	
Weakness	

Beta

_____

_____

_____

_____

Notes

Rock Climbing Log

Date	Time	Name of Climb

Grade	Location	Route	Length

Attempts	Achieved	Partners

Strength	
Weakness	

Beta

_____

_____

_____

_____

Notes

Rock Climbing Log

Date	Time	Name of Climb

Grade	Location	Route	Length

Attempts	Achieved	Partners

Strength	
Weakness	

Beta

_____

_____

_____

Notes

Rock Climbing Log

Date	Time	Name of Climb

Grade	Location	Route	Length

Attempts	Achieved	Partners

Strength	
Weakness	

Beta

_____

_____

_____

_____

Notes

Rock Climbing Log

Date	Time	Name of Climb

Grade	Location	Route	Length

Attempts	Achieved	Partners

Strength	
Weakness	

Beta

_____

_____

_____

_____

Notes

Rock Climbing Log

Date	Time	Name of Climb

Grade	Location	Route	Length

Attempts	Achieved	Partners

Strength	
Weakness	

Beta

_____

_____

_____

Notes

Rock Climbing Log

Date	Time	Name of Climb

Grade	Location	Route	Length

Attempts	Achieved	Partners

Strength	
Weakness	

Beta

_____

_____

_____

_____

Notes

Rock Climbing Log

Date	Time	Name of Climb

Grade	Location	Route	Length

Attempts	Achieved	Partners

Strength	
Weakness	

Beta

_____

_____

_____

_____

Notes

Rock Climbing Log

Date	Time	Name of Climb

Grade	Location	Route	Length

Attempts	Achieved	Partners

Strength	
Weakness	

Beta

_____

_____

_____

Notes

Rock Climbing Log

Date	Time	Name of Climb

Grade	Location	Route	Length

Attempts	Achieved	Partners

Strength	
Weakness	

Beta

_____

_____

_____

_____

Notes

Rock Climbing Log

Date	Time	Name of Climb

Grade	Location	Route	Length

Attempts	Achieved	Partners

Strength	
Weakness	

Beta

_____

_____

_____

Notes

Rock Climbing Log

Date	Time	Name of Climb

Grade	Location	Route	Length

Attempts	Achieved	Partners

Strength	
Weakness	

Beta

_____

_____

_____

Notes

Rock Climbing Log

Date	Time	Name of Climb

Grade	Location	Route	Length

Attempts	Achieved	Partners

Strength	
Weakness	

Beta

_____

_____

_____

_____

Notes

Rock Climbing Log

Date	Time	Name of Climb

Grade	Location	Route	Lenght

Attempts	Achieved	Length

Strength	
Weakness	

Beta

_____

_____

_____

_____

Notes

Rock Climbing Log

Date	Time	Name of Climb

Grade	Location	Route	Length

Attempts	Achieved	Partners

Strength	
Weakness	

Beta

_____

_____

_____

Notes

Rock Climbing Log

Date	Time	Name of Climb

Grade	Location	Route	Length

Attempts	Achieved	Partners

Strength	
Weakness	

Beta

_____

_____

_____

_____

Notes

Rock Climbing Log

Date	Time	Name of Climb

Grade	Location	Route	Length

Attempts	Achieved	Partners

Strength	
Weakness	

Beta

_____

_____

_____

Notes

Rock Climbing Log

Date	Time	Name of Climb

Grade	Location	Route	Length

Attempts	Achieved	Partners

Strength	
Weakness	

Beta

_____

_____

_____

Notes

Rock Climbing Log

Date	Time	Name of Climb

Grade	Location	Route	Length

Attempts	Achieved	Partners

Strength	
Weakness	

Beta

_____

_____

_____

Notes

Rock Climbing Log

Date	Time	Name of Climb

Grade	Location	Route	Length

Attempts	Achieved	Partners

Strength	
Weakness	

Beta

_____

_____

_____

_____

Notes

Rock Climbing Log

Date	Time	Name of Climb

Grade	Location	Route	Length

Attempts	Achieved	Partners

Strength	
Weakness	

Beta

_____

_____

_____

_____

Notes

Rock Climbing Log

Date	Time	Name of Climb

Grade	Location	Route	Length

Attempts	Achieved	Partners

Strength	
Weakness	

Beta

_____

_____

_____

_____

Notes

Rock Climbing Log

Date	Time	Name of Climb

Grade	Location	Route	Length

Attempts	Achieved	Partners

Strength	
Weakness	

Beta

_____

_____

_____

_____

Notes

Rock Climbing Log

Date	Time	Name of Climb

Grade	Location	Route	Length

Attempts	Achieved	Partners

Strength	
Weakness	

Beta

_____

_____

_____

_____

Notes

Rock Climbing Log

Date	Time	Name of Climb

Grade	Location	Route	Length

Attempts	Achieved	Partners

Strength	
Weakness	

Beta

_____

_____

_____

_____

Notes

Rock Climbing Log

Date	Time	Name of Climb

Grade	Location	Route	Length

Attempts	Achieved	Partners

Strength	
Weakness	

Beta

_____

_____

_____

_____

Notes

Rock Climbing Log

Date	Time	Name of Climb

Grade	Location	Route	Length

Attempts	Achieved	Partners

Strength	
Weakness	

Beta

_____

_____

_____

_____

Notes

Rock Climbing Log

Date	Time	Name of Climb

Grade	Location	Route	Length

Attempts	Achieved	Partners

Strength	
Weakness	

Beta

_____

_____

_____

_____

Notes

Rock Climbing Log

Date	Time	Name of Climb

Grade	Location	Route	Length

Attempts	Achieved	Partners

Strength	
Weakness	

Beta

_____

_____

_____

Notes

Rock Climbing Log

Date	Time	Name of Climb

Grade	Location	Route	Length

Attempts	Achieved	Partners

Strength	
Weakness	

Beta

_____

_____

_____

_____

Notes

Rock Climbing Log

Date	Time	Name of Climb

Grade	Location	Route	Length

Attempts	Achieved	Partners

Strength	
Weakness	

Beta

_____

_____

_____

_____

Notes

Rock Climbing Log

Date	Time	Name of Climb

Grade	Location	Route	Length

Attempts	Achieved	Partners

Strength	
Weakness	

Beta

_____

_____

_____

Notes

Rock Climbing Log

Date	Time	Name of Climb

Grade	Location	Route	Length

Attempts	Achieved	Partners

Strength	
Weakness	

Beta

_____

_____

_____

_____

Notes

Rock Climbing Log

Date	Time	Name of Climb

Grade	Location	Route	Length

Attempts	Achieved	Partners

Strength	
Weakness	

Beta

_____

_____

_____

_____

Notes

Rock Climbing Log

Date	Time	Name of Climb

Grade	Location	Route	Length

Attempts	Achieved	Partners

Strength	
Weakness	

Beta

_____

_____

_____

_____

Notes

Rock Climbing Log

Date	Time	Name of Climb

Grade	Location	Route	Length

Attempts	Achieved	Partners

Strength	
Weakness	

Beta

_____

_____

_____

_____

Notes

Rock Climbing Log

Date	Time	Name of Climb

Grade	Location	Route	Length

Attempts	Achieved	Partners

Strength	
Weakness	

Beta

_____

_____

_____

Notes

Rock Climbing Log

Date	Time	Name of Climb

Grade	Location	Route	Length

Attempts	Achieved	Partners

Strength	
Weakness	

Beta

_____

_____

_____

Notes

Rock Climbing Log

Date	Time	Name of Climb

Grade	Location	Route	Length

Attempts	Achieved	Partners

Strength	
Weakness	

Beta

_____

_____

_____

_____

Notes

Rock Climbing Log

Date	Time	Name of Climb

Grade	Location	Route	Length

Attempts	Achieved	Partners

Strength	
Weakness	

Beta

_____

_____

_____

_____

Notes

Rock Climbing Log

Date	Time	Name of Climb

Grade	Location	Route	Length

Attempts	Achieved	Partners

Strength	
Weakness	

Beta

_____

_____

_____

_____

Notes

Rock Climbing Log

Date	Time	Name of Climb

Grade	Location	Route	Length

Attempts	Achieved	Partners

Strength	
Weakness	

Beta

_____

_____

_____

_____

Notes

Rock Climbing Log

Date	Time	Name of Climb

Grade	Location	Route	Length

Attempts	Achieved	Partners

Strength	
Weakness	

Beta

_____

_____

_____

Notes

Rock Climbing Log

Date	Time	Name of Climb

Grade	Location	Route	Length

Attempts	Achieved	Partners

Strength	
Weakness	

Beta

_____

_____

_____

Notes

Rock Climbing Log

Date	Time	Name of Climb

Grade	Location	Route	Length

Attempts	Achieved	Partners

Strength	
Weakness	

Beta

_____

_____

_____

_____

Notes

Rock Climbing Log

Date	Time	Name of Climb

Grade	Location	Route	Length

Attempts	Achieved	Partners

Strength	
Weakness	

Beta

_____

_____

_____

_____

Notes

Rock Climbing Log

Date	Time	Name of Climb

Grade	Location	Route	Length

Attempts	Achieved	Partners

Strength	
Weakness	

Beta

_____

_____
_____

_____

Notes

Rock Climbing Log

Date	Time	Name of Climb

Grade	Location	Route	Length

Attempts	Achieved	Partners

Strength	
Weakness	

Beta

_____

_____

_____

Notes

www.ingramcontent.com/pod-product-compliance
Lightning Source LLC
Chambersburg PA
CBHW030913080526
44589CB00010B/288